soft heart

Tara Kiernan

BookLeaf Publishing

India | USA | UK

Presentation by *BookLeaf Publishing*

Web: www.bookleafpub.com

E-mail: info@bookleafpub.com

ISBN: 9789357618595

First edition 2023

soft hearts need air and fire
thank you for fanning the flames

poetry for the soft hearts looking for inspiration, fuming with anger, struggling in despair, and searching for connection.

Harden

I am tough
My dad raised me so
But I am also soft
As my mom knows
The battering of the outside
Ensures a tougher shell
It will be harder to see me
And I'll leave you to your hell
But truly raging inside
Is a fire of righteous degree
When all I really wanted
Was to be there for your need
So continue to make me tougher
At your own expense
I'll save these warm embers
For one worthy, less dense

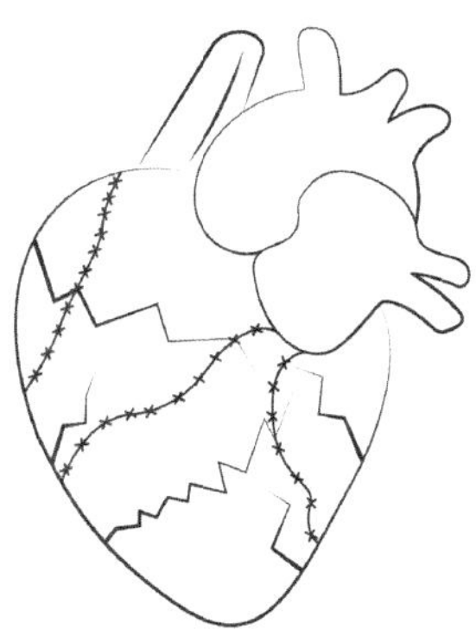

Ashes

Stop pushing me
Stop shoving me
Stop hinting at stupidity

Stop the abusing
Stop the accusing
Stop your attempt
To be controlling

Stop reminding me I'm wrong
Stop saying your right
Stop telling me to come
Toward the light

Stop playing the master
Stop making me the puppet
I'm not a treasure
You can covet

Just Stop Just Stop
Just leave it alone
You bring it up
Like I want it known

Stop blaming
Stop claiming
Stop whatever you were saying

Stop walking the walk
Stop talking the talk
Everything you say is bought

Stop it Drop it
Just leave it alone
You bring it up
Like I need it known

Riser

On a sinking ship, with those I love
Disappears beneath, and pulls us down
We fight the fluid, keep our heads above
We fight each other, don't want to drown
I struggle to breathe, help I seek
But they turn to me, struggle and cling
This can't be it, seems all so bleak
They want this help, I cannot bring
What do I do, our time grows small
I can't give up, I can't be done
Quickly think, can I save us all
For, them, I love, I won't lose one
I delve deep, inside of me
Immerse myself into the heat
I feel the person, I can be
Brush the strength, that's now in need
Grab a hold, of lives I love
Cannot fail now, too much at stake
It's all or no one, we rise above
Our unity, no thing can take.

I am drowning beneath the ice
On a pocket of air I breathe
I need someone to break me free
Any kind of help would suffice
Trapped below this sheet of glass, I
Watch the ones I love grow scared
With horror, let them know I cared
They cannot hear my screams and cries
Their fear reflects the panicked scene
The cold consumes my existence
I succumb to its persistence
They beat upon the ice for me
I do not feel an ounce of heat
I cannot think, I only hurt
My blood, so cold, no longer burns
My heart I feel is losing beat
My senses, gone, can't feel my flesh
I'll cease to be, forevermore
If they cannot save me before
It eats away, I freeze to death.

Below

To Come

Beautiful girl, toenails painted red
    With brunette curls piled atop your head
Eyes so deep, deep blue seas
    Windows to the soul, full of glee
Your smile, amazing, lights a room
    Though imperfect, holds no gloom
Your body is special, love your skin
    Work of art, masterpiece you're in
You know your place, where you stand
    Hopes and dreams held in your hand
Independent, all on your own
    Yet, always able, to find home
Some day, a life, you will brush
    They'll live solely to feel your touch
Upon this sight, your heart will leap
    This knight should sweep you off your feet
There may be others along the way
    But don't just settle, don't fall astray
        They will be the one to give their heart,
        They'll steal yours, and you'll not part

Fly

On the ground,
I was found,
A caterpillar,
Small and round.

From the ground,
I would cry,
When I would try,
To touch the sky.

You saw my dreams,
To touch the sky,
You gave me wings,
To fly so high.

From caterpillar,
You helped me change,
Metamorphosis,
Change with age.

Butterfly,
Fly so high,
Grab the wind,
Touch the sky.

To Mom and Dad

On my first day
I was laid in your arms
I knew you were there
To protect me from harm
  And I was yours
In my first week
We bonded fast
I needed and annoyed you
As the novelties passed
  And I was yours
In my first month
My senses soared
You showed me everything
You helped me explore
  And I was yours
In my first year
Chubbiness near gone
I was learning to walk
But I still held on
  And I was yours
When I took my first fall
You ran to me
Scooped me up
Kissed my knee
  And I was yours
When I came across
My very first bind
I ran to you

For peace of mind
  And I was yours
When my heart
Began to seek
There you were
With answers to speak
  And I was yours
As years passed
You'd still gaze in
My big blue eyes
Mischievous grin
You were there
But now I am grown
I face my problems
All on my own
We are best friends
We still have that bond
We started as
I was laid in your arms
I still talk to you
About my life
What's going well
What's causing strife
I will always
Find my way
Back to your arms
Where I stay
  I will always be yours.

Prelude

Show me why you need me,
Tell me that you care,
Show me how you want me,
Tell me what you dare.

I need you like air,
You make me feel alive,
Alone I'm in despair,
Because of you I thrive.

I love it that you need me,
I love it how you care,
But I'd love to have you show me,
Show me how you dare.

Domino

Pay it forward
You know the game
Just give back
Take your aim

Do something good
For a stranger
Even a friend
Where's the danger

May be failure
But worth a try
Effects can last
After you die

Lend a hand
The world can change
Sometimes it takes one
Link the chain.

Purpose

12

What's the point?

Why do we keep on treading this beaten path?

Do we search for meaning?

Or are we clones on a mechanical wrath?

The sun sets on us all. So does this life we lead

Leave anything behind?

A preacher brings 'light', and the cop gives safety to our lives.

Does that mean they found reasoning in theirs?

Anyone else feel useless?

Why do we fight and wage such wars?

We're stuck here together and life's too short.

So what comes next?

We breathe in, breathe out.

Like clocks wound up.

Tick tock, tick tock.

They say life's greatest happiness,

Is to love and be loved,

But what do we do 'til we find it?

And what if it never comes?

Lesson

If I had to say what I've learned from you
I'd have to say it's something on quitting
Before I would ever call myself through
I would give it my hardest hitting
But no, not you. You'd go without a fight
But it's ok because I see from your life
Why you have faltered and failed
I just don't see why you've been bailed
I understand why you see no reason to try
When you truly believe all is lost
But if ever an ounce of hope were mine
And the smallest chance, my way, was tossed
Then, being stronger than you, I'd give my all
And I'd still be fearless should I ever fall.

Essence

I told my sage once
　That a puzzle my heart is
And every person in my life
　Was a piece that fit.
I said how each piece
　Held its one place
Making up my heart
　Interlocking with grace.
But in the very middle
　There was a vacancy
Awaiting the one person
　for whom it was meant to be.
So now I roll you over
　Feel every edge of you
Inspect where it is you fit
　And if it can be true.

Action

Maybe love is greater than hate
But when one leads the other, follows mistakes
When a boy avenges a brother
A son serves for a mother
Reasons unknown, for one blinds the other
Driven cosmically, a storm blots the sun
Parting sweetly, once the damage is done
To err is human, how 'bout forgive
On this path of destruction no one can live
A world of fighting, and all for what
Toddlers over a toy, it's time to grow up
We'll all join hands, once it's too late
We'll block out the sun, and beg for a better fate.

Pillar

I'm tired of being vile
But I'm sick of being hurt
I either seal myself up
Or keep
getting burned
So why
keep living
When I'm this
shut down
Such an
evil spirit
Walking
the ground
But you're
the best thing
In life
I've found
So I hold
on to you
Hold on
so tight
Please hold
on to me
With all
your might
Don't let me go
Keep me in this fight
Don't let me slip away
Hold me in your light.

We're raised in this world,
Blindfolded and Dumb,
An **ARMY OF STUPID**,
Unaware is each one.
When you're brought into the light,
And shown your true ways,
I hope that you find,
The doom in your days.
To call yourself human,
Is nothing to honor,
Leeches of life,
You feed off each other.
To say we are fittest,
Intellectually advanced,
Is narcissistic,
An arrogant trance.
On this paved path,
There comes a day,
When blindfolds are off,
Alibis thrown away.
You discover this world,
So fueled by hate,
You fall in the ranks,
File through the gate.
There is no escaping,
Some think they can change,
But it's the nature of human,
Destruction's the game.

Angel

Here lives a dog
Spoiled and rotten
Fed very well
And never forgotten
She's so content
Living here
Always knowing
We're somewhere near
Nose to the ground
Tail to the sky
On a trail
Singing high
But what makes this bond
So very special
The love we share
Is unconditional.

Skirmish

Backs to the dirt, bound with braces
Cold metal chains, fear in their faces
This isn't where any of them belong
They are the right, the true, and strong
The captors, so cruel, spit and taunt them
If they get out alive, it'll forever haunt them
But I've had enough, set the noble aside
Follow me through; I'll be your guide
I'd expect it too, when I am in need
For someone to lead, no matter what be
So get off your knees, stand tall on your feet
We'll fight for the weak, 'til they too are free
Set your own life aside, and swallow your pride
Make selfless implied, give it undenied
Now the winds of change are blowing
Enemies' eyes are wide with knowing
We came this time to fight to the death
Give it all you've got, I'll give my last breath.

Corona

You gave me a halo
And softened my wings
You showed me the good
This life can bring
But now you should know
And I've waited so long
I'm everything bad
Now that you're gone
You fed me lies
Poisoned my ear
I know what you were
And want you to fear
The hole you left
Can't be undone
You blew me apart
Left me bitter and numb
Now I return the favor
To everyone around
Give them a taste
Of what threw me down
I ripped off the halo
And burned off the wings
After they soaked
In sin and gasoline

The pain wasn't hard
No not after you
These wounds healed fast
Easy to cover, too
But the hole in my chest
Is black and rotten
The venom surges
With past unforgotten
It soaked me through
With a blood so black
And I embraced it
No turning back
Of the scars from my wings
I am not ashamed
I'll never fly again
And you're to blame
So I tossed the halo
And singed the wings
Soaked in hate
And gasoline

Descendent

I wanted to spend time with you
I wanted to know your past
I wanted to ask so many things
Why couldn't your fire last?

I've heard many times said to me
How much I look and act like you
I wish I could have known myself
But I still hope it's true

When I think I've forgotten your face
I cling tight to the photos
But there are things they can't tell me
I guess things I'll never know

Succumb

I fend off the lonely
Day by day
By keeping busy
I keep it away
But when setting sun
Ends the day
Lonely creeps into dreams
And there it stays.

Rhythm

Sometimes I wonder
If other people listen
Are led by their heart
Instincts and intuition
For I have no problem
Mine can be quite clear
They help steer my course
Should I simply lend an ear
Next time you are lost
Search for answers within
Listen to your instincts
To find your path again.

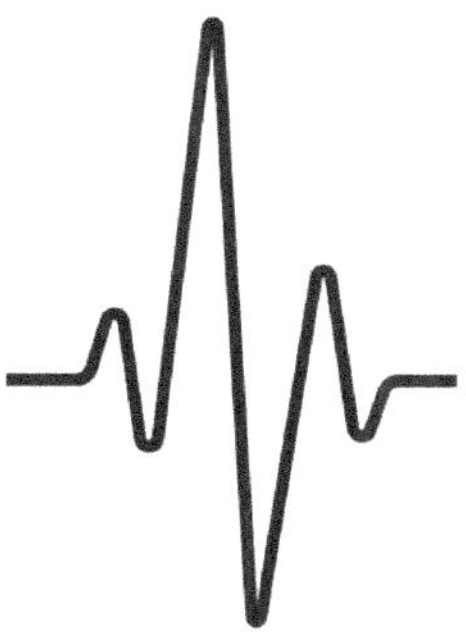

9 789357 618595